"The words just jump off the pages as if you are having a one on one conversation with Shar McBee. For the maximum impact from the book, do the exercises she suggests at the end; they'll help to gel what you glean from the pages."

Rebecca Henderson
Book Reviewer and Columnist

"A plain and simple guidebook for managers. Especially recommended for anyone recently promoted to a managerial or leadership position in the workplace."

Midwest Book Review
Publisher of book review magazines and library newsletters

"The book had a 'spiritual' and 'joyful' element that made me feel more balanced after reading it. The advice is powerful and doable. The day after reading this book, I had a meeting with a 'difficult' board member. Thinking about giving her something rather than thinking about how to make her change her annoying behavior made me deal with her differently. The meeting went well and I feel we know each other better as people."

Francine Christiansen
Past President of the Junior League of Hartford, CT

"What a gift this book offers; and in such a powerful way with the beautiful stories so well written."

Inese Kaufman
President, ICS Consulting Group

JOY OF
LEADERSHIP

JOY OF LEADERSHIP

The Only Secret to Your Success as a New Leader

SHAR McBEE

PUBLISHING, INC.

DEDICATED TO ALL NEW LEADERS
WITH SPECIAL GRATITUDE TO ONE

SMB Publishing, Inc.
www.JoyofLeadership.com

Design by Paul Van Deusen
with inspiration from Richard Laeton
Cover photo by Susan Bransfield
Editor Terry Hiller
Copyeditor Jose Mestre

Printed in the United States of America.
ISBN 0-9638560-6-5

ACKNOWLEDGMENTS

On a beautiful Fall day, a group of friends and experts gathered around my fireplace and we discussed leadership. My deep gratitude to those who attended plus all who explored these values with me, read the manuscript, and offered your insightful comments: Tim Barnett, Matt Barziza, Tim Benson, Bonnie Callens, Dyan Campbell, Benjamin Cardenas, Rolinda Carrington, Mary Castleberry, Edna Ching, Francine Christiansen, Garrick Colwell, Deborah Dewitt, Savi Ermini, Catherine Ertelt, Cindy Franklin, Devika Follosco, Gail Forrest, Delia Grigsby, Kathy Harkins, Rebecca Henderson, Arnie Herz, Cathy Herzog, Terri Jessup, Hugh Johnson, Inese Kaufman, Mary Lange, Bette Lawrence, Geoff Lindsey, Mac Littlefield, Shyamala Littlefield, Mohammad Marashi, Mary Lou McCombie, Erika Nessier, Arline Oberst, Elizabeth O'Connor, Paula Pustmueller, Joanna Rachins, Joy Rodino, Rita Ross, Nancy Shafer, Osnat Shurer, Michelle Seto, Jonathan Star, Betsy Strick, Veronica Tao, Gina Truex, George Weiss, Joyce Wells and Marie Zayc.

Thank you to Robert G. Allen and Joycebelle Edelbrock for the way you generously shared your "Info-preneuring" expertise.

TABLE OF CONTENTS

BEFORE YOU BEGIN

In the end, it's not the years
in your life that count.
It's the life in your years.

Abraham Lincoln

A great life is made up of great moments. *Joy of Leadership* will quickly transform your ordinary moments into great moments, and your life into a great life.

Joy of Leadership is natural leadership. It is based on nature's effortless flow. Once you get into the flow, you thrive. Your work becomes easier. People want to join you. You are rewarded immeasurably.

In *Joy of Leadership* you will learn a secret – the only secret that you need to be successful as a new leader. Once you learn it, your leadership will be as natural as a flowing river. You will know how to give like nature gives and how to receive as much as nature receives. Let's say you have one avocado seed. If you plant it, nature doesn't give you back one avocado. It gives you back *thousands* of avocados. Still, you must know how to plant the seed. If you hold on to your seed and don't plant it, you'll lose the thousands of avocados that would naturally come to you.

Many leadership books are written by titans of industry. This one isn't. Perhaps like you, my earliest experiences of leadership were in school – as a class president, then a cheerleader, later organizing volunteers.

Leadership has never been a career move for me. It's been a call of the heart. I organized the largest voter registration drive in the history of California after seeing how disenfranchised the poor are. I led a class for pregnant high school girls when I heard that 90% of the people in jail were born to teenaged mothers.

I never planned to be a leader. I just said, "Yes," when asked and, again and again, found myself being promoted. Then one day, without any management training, I was put in charge of supervising a staff of 500 people.

It was difficult.

In the beginning, a good word to describe me would have been *cunning.* When I needed help, I thought I had to con people or trick them to do the work. When I needed something, I thought I had to "get" it. The more I tried to "get," the more I suffered. It was painful when people didn't show up or didn't cooperate. Sometimes they would run away when they saw me coming. Or worse, criticize and gossip about me.

Being the leader was not fun.

Then a wonderful mentor taught me a leadership secret that turned everything around. Unexpectedly, serving as the leader became delightful.

When I applied what I learned, difficulties made me creative rather than impotent. When others didn't see things my way, I could detach from the dilemma and see obstacles as opportunities. When a road seemed blocked, a new road became visible. I was amazed at my staff's enthusiasm and how easy it became to attract people to join in.

I wrote a book to inspire volunteer leaders: *To Lead is to Serve.* As a result, I was asked to speak at conventions. We made video and audio tapes to sell. Even though it was written for volunteers, Shell Oil bought the book for use in a corporate situation. The Independent Bankers Association of Texas bought twenty-five copies for leadership training. General Colin Powell sent me a handwritten letter saying he believed in the title. President George W. Bush even quoted my book on television.

Suddenly, I was in business. It was then I recognized firsthand how the secret I learned as a volunteer leader will work wonders for commercial ventures, too.

WHY THIS BOOK IS SHORT

When I was a new leader, I didn't have time to read management books. Hundreds of people were asking me questions and expecting quick decisions. The advice I needed may have been available, but I didn't have time to search for it. I could barely keep my head above water. That's why this book is short. It holds one secret I learned from my mentor that made all the difference in the world.

There are elements of leadership that can be challenging for anyone and especially for a new leader: team building, public speaking, motivating your staff, managing multiple tasks and succeeding at your mission. All of these challenges can be addressed using one secret. It worked for me and it will work for you, too.

The advice in *Joy of Leadership* is simple. It will not cost you time. You do not have to spend your money. All you have to do is make a small shift. Just as a tiny shift at the axis produces a huge increase in a wheel's power, a small shift in your perspective can make the difference between failure and success.

The shift is so small that it would be easy to discount its value. Don't! Big results, life-changing results, often come from taking small actions.

When the solution is simple,
God is answering.

Albert Einstein

A long row of cages lined the walls of the animal shelter where I went to pick out a kitten. Each one held many cats. As I walked the row, suddenly a tiny gray paw reached through the bars and grabbed hold of my gray cashmere sweater. I tried in vain to extricate myself but the determined kitten refused to let go. Eventually I surrendered: "Okay, you're the one."

Now, when I watch my cat lounging curled up in front of the fireplace, I marvel at the results she got from that one deed. It only took a moment. She knew what she wanted and went for it. One small action changed the course of her entire life. So never discount the value of small actions.

An old joke quips, "Tell people there are 900 billion stars and they believe you. Tell them a bench has wet paint and they have to touch it." In the same way, it may be easier to sell a complicated idea than to convince people to try a simple solution.

This leadership method is not complicated. It's a simple solution. Because it is based on the laws of nature, *Joy of Leadership* is easy to comprehend. You don't have to learn a new language to understand and apply the secret. Once you discover it, it will help you find your way through leadership – and life – joyfully.

It is said that if you want to find out about people, give them a little power. What they do with their power will reveal everything. We've all seen leaders become inflated with ego, self-importance and pride. You won't, because the *Joy of Leadership* method will prevent you from becoming arrogant.

A joyous leader has a generous heart. Employing the secret will make it easy for you to laugh and say, "Yes!" Your happiness will have a unifying effect on the people around you, which could win you more far-reaching support than you have ever expected, needed, or imagined.

All things come to the person
who is modest and kind
in a high position.

I Ching

Benjamin Franklin said, "Three may keep a secret if two of them are dead." This secret is not one to keep.

After you learn – and benefit from – the *Joy of Leadership* secret, this is what I hope you will do with it:

- ❧ You will support associates when they take on leadership roles.

- ❧ You will teach the secret to others so that they, like you, can work with people and thrive.

- ❧ Finally, I hope you'll use the secret to transform new managers into joyous leaders, moments into great moments, and your life into a great life.

HOW TO BE SUCCESSFUL: BE GIVING

One day, as I was leaving a library, I noticed an attractive table set up with food, drinks, and a vase of colorful flowers. It was quite eye-catching, so I asked the librarian, "Are you having a party?"

"No," she responded, "A meeting."

"That looks elaborate for a meeting," I commented.

Then the librarian responded with something I'll never forget. She said, "If you need them, feed them."

This librarian understood a basic tenet of happiness and success: If you give first, people want to give back to you. They want to reciprocate. She was going to ask the people who attended the meeting for something. But before she asked, the librarian first gave out refreshments.

Whatever you desire, the moment you begin giving you open yourself to receive it.

If you want your staff to respect you, give them respect. If you want your employees to value your leadership, first value them. If you want to be a joyful leader, give your joyfulness. Whenever you want anything from people, first be giving and they'll want to give back to you.

Diane supervises a staff of 540 people. As you can imagine, there is a lot of demand for her time and attention. Her secretary wasn't screening calls or shielding her from interruptions. "I wish she would take some initiative," Diane said. "My assistant isn't assisting me. She's not much help and I'm frustrated."

Then Diane took one of my seminars where we discussed the point, "If you want to be happy, be giving." Diane wasn't happy. She was grumbling. She was right about her secretary. The woman wasn't helpful. However, Diane decided that rather than be right, she'd like to be happy.

She spent a lunch hour asking herself, "What can I give to my secretary?" Diane came up with a few ideas and had not implemented even one when, she said, "The most amazing thing happened. That afternoon my secretary worked like a maniac for me all afternoon. She called 45 people. Left messages. Wrote little notes to me about each one she reached. It was an awesome change."

A famous author once asked, "Do you have to give before you can receive?" It's an interesting question, isn't it? The answer is like the proverbial chicken and the egg.

Diane hadn't overtly given anything. She had only made an intention to give when her secretary began giving to her.

It is in giving that we receive.

St. Francis of Assisi

How do you separate the light from the lamp? The fragrance from the flower? Where does one end and the other begin? In the same way, how do you separate giving from receiving? Giving and receiving are both part of a natural cycle. They are one. When you give, you enter the naturally abundant cycle of life and you open yourself to success and achievement.

When I was an entertainment reporter in Hollywood, I interviewed almost every rock star, movie star, and television star who was famous at that time. When I interviewed new stars – celebrities with a first best-selling album or first starring role – they wanted to talk about their careers. But when I interviewed established stars who had lots of hits, they often avoided talking about their success. Instead, they wanted to tell me about their philanthropy.

Bono is a great example. This Irish rock star became a huge success with his band U2, and what is he most proud of? His work for the people in Africa. Dolly Parton, one of the most successful country western entertainers of all time, told me her voice was a gift from God and she only wanted to use it to give back. Comedian Jerry Lewis and his decades of work for the telethon for Muscular Dystrophy is another example. For these stars, being rich and famous wasn't enough. Stardom and receiving adulation didn't give them complete joy. What made them truly happy was giving to others.

Over the years I have seen how giving brings amazing results. I saw it help an advertising firm hold on to a good employee, a church increase its members, and a soccer coach turn a losing team into a winner. The list goes on.

Opera diva Beverly Sills spoke in New York City at the 100-year anniversary of the Junior League. I was in the audience when she related an experience about being asked to serve on several boards of directors. Each group assured her that she wouldn't have to do anything. They insisted, "All you have to do is let us use your name."

Sills declined each invitation. Then one group said, "You'll have to work hard for us. We want a lot from you." To them she said, "Yes." She had a lot to give and she wanted to give it. Giving made her happy. Many organizations missed that point and they missed out on having the famous diva as their spokesperson.

DO YOU WANT TO BE HAPPY?

If you want to be happy,
be giving.

Upanishads

Have you ever panicked as a public speaker? Or felt anxious talking before a group? The principle of giving has been enormously valuable to me in public speaking. If I hold the thought, "I am here to give," it wards off fear and frees my communication to come from the heart.

But sometimes I forget...

Once I was speaking to a banquet hall full of Lutheran ministers and lay ministers when, suddenly, I panicked. A wave of doubt engulfed me. I thought, "How can I inspire them? Surely they must be better speakers than me. What could they possibly learn?"

As I began to falter, the man who had hired me to speak, Bill, looked worried.

Miraculously, at that point I remembered, "If you want to be happy, be giving." This advice has made a wonderful difference in my life. Couldn't I just share what I know?

Fear evaporated as I began to focus on giving to the audience. It no longer felt like I was standing before a crowd of skilled experts who were judging me. I could see the faces of the people I was speaking to, look into their eyes, and share from my heart. Bill relaxed. So did I!

The next time you dread giving a speech, or feel anxious making an announcement before a group, try the "giving" formula. Magic occurred that day when I moved the focus off of myself and onto the audience. The situation became comfortable when I stopped worrying, "What are they thinking of me?" and started asking, "What can I offer these people?"

It's not a coincidence that we use the phrase, "*Giving* a speech." Choosing to be giving saved me that day with the ministers and has saved me with hundreds of other audiences since.

The dramatic change neither cost me money nor extra time. All I had to do was make the small shift from, "How can I get their approval?" to "What can I give?" I moved from "get" to "give." That simple shift transformed my fear into joy and made all the difference in the world. If you want to be happy, be giving.

Have you ever tried to give something to people who would not accept it? You know they need it. They may even want it. Yet they are not ready to receive it.

Dutch businessman Auke van Keulen was managing a cheese factory in Holland when he discovered that ten percent of the employees couldn't read. Of 300 people, 30 couldn't understand written directions.

"They were smart so they were smart at hiding it," Auke says. "Still, problems of miscommunication were creeping in." Safety became a concern at the plant. So he offered a reading course.

No one signed up. He asked why. No response. Finally, one man privately admitted that he was afraid of telling his children that he couldn't read.

Auke became even more determined. He applied for and received a grant to pay for an in-depth course. Then he held a meeting of the entire staff.

"If individuals can't read, it will hold us back," he explained. "People could get hurt." He asked his literate employees if they would help the illiterate ones. The grant would pay them for their time.

"In only three years, everyone in the factory could read," Auke says. "Normally it takes five years or more for adults to learn to read. It was a victory that brought our team together. Every employee felt responsible for our success."

The manager made it possible for the employees to give to each other. Not only did it make them happy and protect everyone from a potential danger, when people began giving to each other it united the team. Most new managers think that their responsibility is to get people to do a job. Actually, you'll accomplish more if you see your responsibility as making it possible for people to give as much as they can give.

DO YOU WANT YOUR LIFE TO BE BALANCED?

Of all the things I've lost, I miss my mind the most.

Mark Twain

When you give, remember to give to yourself, too. A joyous leader lives a balanced life. This is not selfish; it is a law of nature. If you can't breathe, what can you do for others? If you are burned out and exhausted, what do you have to offer?

The act of giving can be intoxicating. It fills you with magnetism, courage, and joy. People want to join you. New opportunities open up. All of this presents fresh challenges. As your work expands, you may "need" more people to help. You may "need" more money, and you may "need" more time. Beware of becoming needy. If you become needy, instead of being generous, you may begin to feel overwhelmed. When this happens, no one wants to join you. In fact, you become so off balance that people run away from you.

To live a balanced life, learn to give to yourself, too.

I have a friend in Beverly Hills, Fred Nicholas. He builds shopping centers, collects art, and volunteers for innumerable civic activities. He founded Public Counsel, the largest pro bono (not for profit) law firm in the world. He was Chairman of the Los Angeles Museum of Contemporary Art. He was Chairman of the Walt Disney Concert Hall while it was being constructed. It is possible that the term "go-getter" was created to describe this generous man.

I asked, "How do you get so much done and keep your life balanced?"

"Compartmentalize," Fred says, "I compartmentalize my time and my energies. I try to concentrate on one thing at a time. If I have a lot of things that are happening in my life, which is true all the time, I usually get up in the morning and go swimming. I think about the various things I have to deal with, and then I tell myself to take one at a time. Ignore everything else. Concentrate on one thing and try to resolve that. When it is finished, then go on to the next issue."

Compartmentalizing prevents you from becoming flustered. Juggling several projects in your mind can be confusing. So develop the ability to think about only one thing at a time. Practice concentration and discipline.

If you have a lot of enthusiasm, you need to compartmentalize that, too. The rush of a thousand ideas can be overwhelming. People become exhausted by their own enthusiasm. So channel your energy in one direction.

Fred says, "If things are bothering me, I turn them off and then turn them on when it's time to face them."

I asked, "How do you do *that*?"

He said, "Concentration. I've done it for so long that it's a technique I'm familiar with. It's worth learning because it gives you an opportunity to preserve your strength and energy. In the long run, you get more done."

A businesswoman gave me the same advice as Fred. This woman started her own brokerage company and built it into a two-billion-dollar business within ten years.

I asked, "How do you deal with the million issues that must come up in a two-billion-dollar business?"

"Don't deal with a million issues," she said. "Focus. Deal with one issue at a time."

For you, is leadership a sprint or are you in it for the long run? Are you a politician or a stateswoman? Do you want to shoot up fast like a weed and burn out early? Or do you want to make a lasting impact, like a tall tree, visible from afar?

If you are in it for the long run, balance is essential. Otherwise, how will you endure?

*The difference between a politician
and a statesman is this:
The former is concerned with the next
election, while the latter is concerned
with the next generation.*

Will Rogers

Our Dutch friend who started the reading program for his employees, Auke van Keulen, says, "People will stay with your company longer if you create a balanced atmosphere."

Later in his career, Auke became the European Operations Director of the Old El Paso Division for Pillsbury. The average length of employment in that industry is two to three years. Auke's people stayed an average of six to seven years. During his tenure the business grew 50-60% annually and expanded from 35 to 200 employees.

"My challenge was to balance the big push for production and profit coming from the multinational corporation with the needs of each individual. It was important to take the time to walk around and talk about things like soccer to the people I worked with."

Auke says, "Once we had twenty people in the canteen talking about dealing with the death of dear ones and our own fears about dying. We had very open discussions about many subjects right in the middle of a business setting. People valued that highly."

His company's fast growth was stressful for everyone. As the leader, Auke focused on supporting people so they could get the job done. They worked 10 to 12-hour days, so he brought in massage therapists. They went to employees' workstations, set up a chair and gave relaxing neck and shoulder massages.

He told his employees, "I can't solve the problem of stress for you, but we want to give you an experience of what it feels like to be relaxed." Auke says, "After that, many of them started exercising again and the outcome was that our sickness rate decreased rapidly."

Auke advises, "The key is to give people your attention. They worked hard for me, not for Pillsbury. The relationship with the immediate supervisor is the one that counts."

We make a living by what we get.
We make a life by what we give.

Winston Churchill

DO YOU WANT TO PROSPER AND THRIVE?

THREE LAWS OF GIVING

A joyous leader will prosper and thrive naturally. There are three laws of giving that can help you flourish. When you work and live by these laws your life will be balanced and you'll experience the true joy of leadership. Each is a spiritual law. Each is a social law. Each is a law of nature. They've been tried and tested throughout the ages. They've brought success to millions of people and they can bring success to you, too.

1

WHATEVER YOU GIVE COMES BACK MULTIPLIED

In the introduction to this book, an example is made of an avocado seed. If you plant an avocado seed, the tree doesn't give back one avocado. It gives back thousands of avocados – so many that you may not know what to do with them.

The Bible says, "As you sow, so shall you reap." In school I had a teacher who quoted this verse to every kid who misbehaved in class. She used that verse like a threat. In those days I interpreted it to mean that if you are bad, something bad is going to happen to you. Since then, I've learned that the verse does not imply good or bad. It's merely a statement of fact.

If you plant an avocado seed, you grow avocados. If you plant a bitter melon seed, you grow bitter melons. Every time you speak a word or think a thought, you are planting a seed which someday will sprout.

When Arjun Rich was a poor kid growing up in the Bronx, he walked past Trump Tower on Fifth Avenue in New York City and shouted, "That's for me." He said what he wanted. He sowed the seeds of "A nice home is for me." Sure enough, today he owns a beautiful apartment there.

I met Arjun because he shares his good fortune. From time to time he allows volunteer organizations to hold events in his home. I attended two of these occasions, which is how I heard his story.

Another way to understand this law is to look at a circle and consider the phrase, "What goes around comes around." This statement reflects a universal truth. So give what you want to come back to you, because it will.

If you want to be a joyful leader, express your cheerfulness. If you repeat over and over, "My work is discouraging," that is what you will get – a discouraging job. Your employees will be discouraged, too. According to the law of giving, whatever you give comes back multiplied, so laugh while you are at work today and see what happens.

Cynthia Evans, who I enjoyed working with in Australia, told me that she likes to work alone. She's not keen on group assignments. Then, one day, she was promoted to the position of department head. She thought, "In order to survive, I have to make this fun." She made an intention to be light-hearted. She determined that she would not allow herself to become grave with responsibilities.

"It worked," she says, "Everyone who was involved loved working on that project."

Then, because Cynthia was successful, she was put in charge of another project. This time she forgot her intention. She wanted to work in a joyful atmosphere, but she didn't plan for it. She jumped into the new endeavor without remembering to make an intention to be light-hearted.

Cynthia says, "I felt burdened and that rubbed off on all the others. It was a disappointing experience."

It takes concerted effort to live a joyful life. To be happy requires an intention to be so. It doesn't happen by accident. It takes consistent determination. Remember this when you are the leader, for the spotlight is on you. Whatever attitude you exude will come back to you because whatever you give comes back multiplied.

*To everything there is a season
and a time for every purpose
under heaven.*

Ecclesiastes

2

TO EVERYTHING
THERE IS A SEASON

Whatever we give will come back to us, although we can't control when. We can ask for a specific date, but we can't dictate it. You can plant a seed, but you can't be sure when it is going to sprout.

My Aunt Lois was the oldest of five daughters. When Lois was 15 years old her father died suddenly. He was a pharmacist in a small town in Texas. After he was gone, the family couldn't sell the pharmacy and it went out of business. Suddenly my grandmother had no income and six mouths to feed. She did what many widows in those days did. She rented bedrooms in her home to boarders. Still, the family needed more income to make ends meet.

Aunt Lois quit school and went to work as a bookkeeper in the town's only movie theater. She promised to work until her younger sisters finished high school.

Aunt Lois was 29 years old when her last sister graduated. The next day, Aunt Lois boarded a train for California to marry her sweetheart who had been waiting for her. She never graduated from high school but she did become a successful seamstress, creating costumes for movie stars such as Barbra Streisand in *Hello Dolly* and television shows like *M.A.S.H.*

When Aunt Lois was 88, she fell and broke her hip. By then, her husband and all of her sisters were deceased. She needed help. So I moved from Honolulu, Hawaii, to Austin, Texas, to care for her. She lived with me for the last five years of her life.

I love the quote from Ecclesiastes, "To everything there is a season," because it reminds me of Aunt Lois. When we give, it will come back to us even though we cannot know how, when, or from whom. Aunt Lois' life is a beautiful example of the law of giving. Lois' sisters did not repay her directly for the sacrifice she made for them. But when she needed help, the help was there. She lived a life of giving and when she could no longer give, her past giving supported her. Her gift came full circle years later.

We choose our joys and sorrows long before we experience them.

Kahlil Gibran

3

THE KEY TO GIVING
IS TO GIVE A SEED

When Mark Twain was asked what he
thought of Richard Wagner's music, he said,
"It's not as bad as it sounds." When you
suggest to people that they be giving,
sometimes they don't like the way that sounds.
They may even panic.

"I can't give more. I'm already giving so
much," they cry.

What we learn from nature is that you
don't have to give "so much." Just give a
seed. A seed is a little element that
potentially contains the whole tree. You
don't have to give the whole tree. People
with big hearts may want to give everything.
A friend of mine is extremely generous with
everything he has. If he has ten cents, you
get ten cents. Unfortunately, he gives away
the whole tree. He rarely has money for
himself because he hasn't learned that the
key to giving is to give a seed.

At a meeting, I heard a young woman say she feels guilty because she can't give enough. According to the law of giving, you don't have to give a lot. If you cut down your whole tree and plant it in the ground, it doesn't grow. It dies. On the other hand, if you properly plant one seed, it will grow and you'll have more trees.

If you, like the young woman, feel that you don't have enough to give, try giving in small ways. Perhaps your moment for large-scale action has not arrived. A cloud promises moisture long before rain falls. In the same way, in times when you can't produce great effects, you can do things in small doses.

You can use this when you are facing a big task. You might say, "I'm not up for a big task right now, but I can give ten minutes." Ten minutes is doable. It's less daunting than tackling the whole project. Sometimes the ten minutes will stretch into hours. But even when it doesn't, you are still ten minutes ahead on your big task.

One of the most positive people I know is M.I.T. graduate, Dr. Warren Littlefield. One day Mac, as everyone calls him, went to an auditorium in Manhattan only hours before an honored guest was to speak there. He was stunned by what he found. The auditorium looked like a construction site. There was an inch of dust on the floor, saw horses lying around, and muck everywhere. It was only twelve hours before the audience and the speaker would arrive.

When he tells the story, Mac laughs, "The only cleaning person there was one man polishing a piece of brass. The whole place was filthy and he was polishing brass!"

"Oh my!" Mac thought, "It looks like we've got a job to do here. Better get started."

He made some telephone calls asking for help, then said to himself, "Ok, let's do this; let's do whatever needs to be done." He began to clean and gradually people arrived to help. It took them twelve hours, but the auditorium was clean before the program began.

Mac says, "Of course, you need to trust that it can be done. Why would God present you with a task that couldn't be done? Just take one little step at a time."

"How did you feel after your event?" I asked him.

Mac said, "Absolutely wonderful. Overjoyed. When it was over, and it was a success, it was the greatest exhilaration to sit back and say, 'Ah! I'm tired, but it was fabulous!' I didn't want to go home because I felt so marvelous."

Can you see why Mac's attitude inspired cooperation? He gave his own effort which attracted other people to give theirs, too.

The secret to his success was that no one was asked to do "so much." Each was asked to do a little. When I heard this story I could envision people doing the work with great enthusiasm. Big projects are always most successful when a lot of people do a little, as opposed to one or two people doing everything.

DO YOU WANT TO BE
SIGNIFICANT *AND* SUCCESSFUL?

Not only do altruistic actions bring about happiness; they also lessen our experience of suffering.
Our greatest joy comes when we are motivated by concern for others.

The Dalai Lama

If you want to be significant and successful, be giving. In *Joy of Leadership* this means giving with a good motive and from your heart. An impure motive, one that is selfish, can backfire.

Do not give, ever:

ದ   To deceive or exploit

ದ   As a bargain

ದ   Out of guilt

ದ   Because you've been
     manipulated to give

ದ   When the gift is harmful
     to you or to others.

The act of giving is simple and it is subtle. As a leader, you must be very careful not to give inappropriately. For example, feeding candy to a baby may be an easy way to pacify the baby. It may make the child happy momentarily. But it can be harmful to the child's health in the long run.

A pure gift is good for the giver and the recipient. As an employer, impure giving can backfire for both you and your staff member. Giving someone the wrong job or holding on to someone who has outgrown the position damages you and the employee.

A former neighbor of mine is beautiful and bright, but her fear of rejection causes her to freeze every time she looks for work. Consequently, she never applies for anything but low-paying positions. Even though she is obviously overqualified, each new employer is thrilled to hire her. Then the employer gets upset when she becomes bored with the job, quits, and moves on.

Being in a leadership position brings with it important responsibility. Your job is to provide nourishment in every sense of the word. Intellectual and emotional needs must be met, too. If you can't contribute in a beneficial way to someone's life, you don't deserve to have that person as an employee. People spend most of their waking hours on the job. The reward has to be more valuable to them than only the money. If you remain conscious of this fact, your work will be significant and successful. It will bring great happiness to you and to others.

Before I became a reporter covering the entertainment industry in Hollywood, I was a teacher. One night, while I was interviewing people after a Stevie Wonder concert, a young woman approached. When she introduced herself, I recognized her as a former student. She had been pregnant at age 15. In those days, pregnancy forced girls to drop out of school or enroll in a special program. I was her teacher in a special education school.

Now 22 and the mother of a little girl, she had earned a degree in nursing and loved her job. "You told me I could go to college," she said. "No one in my family even graduated from high school and everyone assumed I would drop out, but you encouraged me. Because of that my daughter and I have a good life. Thank you."

Saint Francis said, "It is in giving that we receive." Years earlier I had given this girl a simple gift: encouragement. I had planted a seed in her mind about a college degree. That night at the concert, I got to see the results. My gift – a little encouragement – didn't cost me extra time or money. Yet you can imagine how happy I am for this young woman, can't you? Her success makes me successful, doesn't it? I gave a little and it returned to me as a huge reward.

A great life is made up of great moments. That, my friends, was one of life's great moments.

DID YOU LEARN THE JOY OF LEADERSHIP SECRET?

HAVE YOU DISCOVERED ITS BENEFITS?

EXERCISE FOR SUCCESS

Over the years I have seen people embrace the *Joy of Leadership* philosophy enthusiastically and successfully. For some, the transformation is permanent. Others are energized for awhile and then they return to their old habits. This exercise is for those who want to make a permanent shift.

Life is like a flowing river. You can try to change the direction the water flows but the river will struggle to return to its familiar course. The only way to create a permanent change in a river is to change the riverbed – change the old structure.

To change the course of your life, you have to do more than want to change. You have to create a structure to support your new choice. The purpose of this exercise is to build a new structure so that your life can flow where you want it to go.

1

If you could receive anything you want from being a leader, what would you want? Make a list.

2

Look at your list. What can you give to the people you work with in order to receive what you want? (Remember: You get what you give.) Next to your wish list, for each item write something that you can give.

3

Think of a person who has disappointed you.
What can you give to this person? A small
act of giving could change your relationship.
Remember not to give a gift that is harmful
to you or to others.

4

Make a list of other circumstances in your
leadership and your life that are not going the
way you want them to go. In each situation,
how can you make the small shift from
getting to giving?

*Those who bring sunshine
into the lives of others,
cannot keep it from themselves.*

Sir James Barrie
Author of *Peter Pan*

ABOUT THE AUTHOR

Shar McBee transforms new managers into joyous leaders. Shar had not received any management training when she was put in charge of a staff of 500 people. A wise mentor taught her a secret. She tried it. It worked amazingly. Since then Shar has taught the secret to thousands.

Shar has been an entertainment reporter for CBS News in Hollywood, a teacher and a public relations agent for Phylicia Rashad of the Cosby Show. For ten years, Shar traveled around the world working with organizations in a dozen countries. What she discovered was what makes great individuals great: They live a life of service.

As a keynote speaker, Shar McBee presents refreshing, insightful ideas that energize you to take action. When she is finished speaking, amazing things happen. With an empowered group of people on your side, nothing can stand in your way.

One of Shar McBee's most electrifying keynote speeches is "To Lead is to Laugh."

To learn more about products and services
for individuals and organizations based on
Joy of Leadership, visit

JOYOFLEADERSHIP.COM

FREE BONUS

If you have a PC with broadband,
we have a bonus for you.
You can download a training manual
to an Adobe PDF file and a video to
Windows Media Format.

Joy of Leadership
Training Manual

www.JoyofLeadership.com/manual/

Joy of Leadership
Video

7 minutes

www.JoyofLeadership.com/video/

Printed in the United States of America.